SEVEN WEEKS <---IN---> MEXICO

BUFOGENESIS, BOOK 1

Dedication

Intentional family.
You know who you are.

~~~Seven Weeks In Mexico is a collection of notes taken by psychonaut JXS as he becomes acquainted with the Sonoran Desert Toad, Bufo Alvarius. The toad's venom contains DMT, a naturally occurring entheogen known as the God molecule. The author documents his personal journey as he trips 77 times over the course of seven weeks in Mexico.

~~~

First Edition

December 22, 2018

San Juan, Puerto Rico, USA

KDP ISBN: 9781791801700

www.unitedstatesofme.org

Prologue

In retrospect, I had no idea what I was getting into. I mean, yeah, I knew the science behind smoking the toad venom of bufo alvarius, the Sonoran Desert toad. And I watched video of others doing it. I read testimonials. So I guess I did my homework, which was a good thing, because the actual experience proved to be something, like marriage or war, for which one can only prepare, but never fully ever really be prepared.

Fortunately, I trusted my people, dear friends who saw me disintegrating and stepped in to help me face myself and embrace the ego death experience before I completed my program of self-destruction. I was on the wide road, headed down to destruction, headed for suicide, and an early grave. And now, I've been given a second chance, because I found out I wasn't ready to give up on this life. DMT saved me.

A quick note on the process of smoking dried flakes of bufo alvarius toad venom, which contains a type of DMT, an endogenous psychedelic chemical found in the human brain which is common throughout nature in both plants and animals. This book is not intended to be a guide of any kind, scientific or otherwise, as it merely collects unedited notes I took in Mexico. Rather, I present my story as testimonial evidence, so the reader can follow someone with a little bit of courage taking take great leaps of faith. Make no mistake, this was a terrifying, death-defying experience. The subject is a white male American, age 39, dosing regularly by smoking the entheogen more than 75 times over 7 weeks, with each trip lasting anywhere from 5 minutes to an hour or so. All this was done under the supervision of people with medical training and plenty of psychedelic experience. In other words, do not try this at home or on your own. If you must go, find a guide, and take it slow.

Correspondence

Did your actions lead to the liberation point?
Did dancing with death or abandonment
of all things lead you, my straw man friend,
to any new place, or did you build and
burn yet another potential life story?

How straw does burn.

I remember you fancied yourself
as a potent force, waiting to break out.
I wonder if that vision still holds?

• Omar Thomas •

10.13.18 -- 3 times

Indescribable. Unreal. Breathtaking.

10.14.18 -- 1 time

All the way under. Lost consciousness. Giving up.
Surrendering everything. Death.

I did not expect to wake up.

10.15.18 -- 1 time

I was worried about wasting the smoke at the
beginning…when I should have been concerned
with not wasting any at the end.

Conclusions: Live in the present moment. Be
here now. This is only the beginning. It's a game.
Life is what you can make of it. To feel free is to
be free. There is no escaping reality. The way out
is to go through it all. Trust the process.

10.16.18 -- 1 time

I will forget, until I don't forget. And that's okay.
Everything is just as I left it. Once a day is
enough. Question of now. What to do. No
question, really. Develop your other side, the left
side of awareness, the blind side. Serve the
servants. You cannot have it both ways...or can
you, you don't know. Ignorance. Ignorance is
bliss. No problem. Ignore the present moment.
Let it come to you. Keep your bliss inside, your
pearl of great price, your very own secret, your
private knowledge, awareness of your own
ignorance. It's a game. You are pretending. Play
your part. Act - and act well. Use your manners.
You don't know what anyone else knows. It may
be a new game for you, but it's the oldest game
there is, the game of matter and energy, the
interplay. It's yin and yang. You made your
choice, long ago, or it was made for you. Deal
with it. You are what you are. That is the
doorway, the beginning. Self realization,

acceptance, love. You get to be happy. No trying, just being, here, now. The world is yours. You can do anything. Play nice. Be good. Genesis. Begin. Now. Find your way. Be cool. It's wide open, the future, waiting for you. Tomorrow, repeat the same pattern that got you to this place today. Live by your mantra. Do your best. Build on the basics. Stay humble. Ask for help.

10.17.18 -- day off
Smoke and mushrooms instead.

Different type of learning experience.
Also priceless. Facing fear from another angle.
All doubts must be conquered.
Leave no stone unturned.

Collect the prizes: virtue, humility, courage, experience. See notes. Repeat as needed.

10.18.18 -- 1 time
I died. And 'came back' to life.

Don't draw any conclusions yet.
If you do, be playful, child.

Stick to the present.
What matters now.

Medicine is for the sick.
You are getting well.
Your new attitude is proof.
All around you, evidence.

Fulfill your own prophecy.
Simply begin again, without fear.
This time will be different.
Count on it.

10.19.18 -- day off

10.20.18 -- written 10.21.18

I went too far this time, thank god. Thought it was over, once again. Each time, I seem to die for a little while, bounce back to the present. Many thoughts come and go, rapidly. Your life is not your own. It is for them you live and love. I am like a blind many learning to see in the dark, a lame man giving up his crutches to walk again. After the trip, I stare in the mirror. Music comes from the house, Radiohead, Bjork, Damien Rice, Manchester Orchestra, a playlist they made for me, to help me find myself again. I am the patient here. They are transplanting new soul into me. They are taking the light out of me and then putting it back in. They are purifying my body-mind, redeeming me. I will go through this process and be free, ready to start all over again. My demons will leave me and angels will replace them as my advisors and guides. I wasted the first half of my life. Now I am being given a fresh start.

10.22.18 -- 3 times

Hold onto the other side of awareness. Literally, bring the opposites together, in your body, in your life. Become whole. Unify your self in one body. Fear not the other, the reflection you see. Stay open.

We all come from above, from heaven, and return there when we're done here. Hell is only a temporal state, a place of attachment to material things. Fear of eternal damnation is only a warning, because nothing lasts forever, no thing. We are angels. Someday we will be Gods, but in the end, return to seeds, potentiality.

10.24.18 -- one time

Childhood memories. Staring at the sun. Left eye, open wide. Spiral. Go into the light. Waking up the other side of my awareness. This is the feeling of consciousness.

10.26.18 -- one time

Each trip I seem to pick up where I left off last time and continue the same journey. Voice of consciousness speaks to me. Let the light in, to purify your body/mind from the inside. You don't see matter, you see light reflected. Darkness is nothing to fear; it is only the absence of light.

You knew all this once, but you forgot, because of your appetite, attachment, materialism, sin. Submit to the light. Idea to get naked in the sun. Let the light heal you, from the inside out. Body is a temple of light, built to hold it. We can live on sunlight, by taking it in through the eyes. We are here, learning how to give up the body and die, graduate, rise, fly into the sun, heaven, home, God.

【●】

10.28.18 -- One time

Either/or. You can't do both. Past or future, in the present. Choose, either this life or the next. X marks the spot. Gnostic cross. Hold on to one thing. Once you die to self, you get a new beginning. Live to serve.

I turned myself inside out for you. It wasn't good enough. It was better the last time. I want to switch sides. Hold on to the opposite. Once you die, you come back to life on the other side of ego death. Resurrection metaphor. To be born again, you have to die. Living on the edge of life. One love.

10.30.18 -- One time

Keep the light inside. Don't fear the sun, or anything, or anyone. Universe originates within. Go deeper. Let go. Forget the past. Erase it all. Get born again. Hold to the present. Find the line. Left and right. Black and white. Novelty. Thou shalt not repeat thyself. Keep the new in front of you. Leave the old behind. Be yourself. There is nothing else. Be loyal to the light. See the light in everything. Don't take anything too seriously out here in the matrix of the material world. The beginning and the end lie with you, my friend. Defocus your vision. Withdraw your attention from the five senses. Hold the magic dancing spark of being in your mind's eye. Keep it on the inside, between your heart and mind. This is what it means to be alive. Close your eyes and start living a new life again, as if for the first time. I will fear no darkness. I will embrace change. I will trust my gut instinct. I will love today.

It just gets deeper and deeper.

Every time, I go further.

The assemblage point, moving.

Things do not have to make sense.

We all have the sun in common.

I am not afraid to burn.

Logic is a trap of opposites.

Understand the principles.

Paradoxically, you are light...
but the mind is attached to the body.

Go into the light and be redeemed.

Open heart. Heal. Sun shine in.

I turned myself inside out for you.

It wasn't good enough.

Humble, this time.

Inner child, mine.

Hold onto the present moment.

I do not need to eat or breathe.

Let the body serve the spirit.

I am a child of the sunlight.

Let your thoughts be mine.
Hold the line, in between.

Resolve paradox.

Face fear.

Hold.

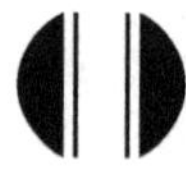

11.02.18 -- 7 times

One time too many, maybe. I saw a place with no light, where even the hope of ever seeing light again was extinguished. It was some kind of death. There is nothing after death, one might conclude. Life and death are opposite sides of the same paradox. Actually, it's both and neither, but that is only the beginning. Every time I think its over, that proves to be untrue. The end is always a new beginning. Each time I die, I get a fresh start, or something.

Childhood memory, running around with blanket over my head, guided by faith, the light inside. It was the shadow of doubt that finally crashed me into something the split my head open. In that moment, around age three, I began to lose my invulnerability. Kicked out of the garden for eating fruit from the forbidden tree, now I have to work to get back to balancing.

More notes from 11.02, recorded 11.03.18:

After smoking the first time, made a 30 minute video, hardly speaking, of myself sitting, breathing and thinking. I felt that the potential audience that might be watching if my phone was hacked would know exactly where I was coming from and be able to read my mind. Many such insights seem fantastical in retrospect - impossible to prove, easy to dismiss. But I remain convinced that these experiences are not only (in a sense) real, as subjective perspectives, parts of a personal history or life story, but are in an objective sense even more real than what we take the world to be. Perception is only a door or a window, opening on a realm which beggars description, a place each one of us must wander through, without a map, a pilgrim's progress, a poet's passage. At first, layers of self are shed, and the smoke pares person down to the core. This process is a thrill. Each time, the subject experiences a new and progressive form of ego death, evolving by leaps and bounds. I am convinced that, is we have souls, or any lasting sense of individuality which transcends the grave, DMT can save us lifetimes of suffering, purify the mind, heal the broken heart and bring karma (action) into focus, aligning thought, word and deed. What has grown crooked can be corrected. There is redemption for the humble sinner even in this very life. And it is not to be found in church, mosque or synagogue, nor in the market place, or the repetition history, or even blessed evolution. The world lies to us, binds the mind and blinds the inner eye. No, redemption for all is in nature, beneath the surface of awareness. Bringing smoke into the body unites spirit with matter at a cellular level. In this way we can reconnect with the source of life which continually gives birth to us, and do so without having to surrender this life and the physical body.

Yoga is the union of apparent opposites, the circling of yin and yang, which are ultimately one thing. After shedding the snake skin of personality, the psychonaut coming out of the experience will be raw, wide open and flexible, ready to be shaped into the very thing she or he always wanted to be anyway. This should be discussed with the tripper before and/or after smoking.

It is worth asking how much preparation a client should be given, what information are they given before and what is held until after. I want to know how much structure a facilitator gives to a tripper, especially a first-timer. My own experience tells my I can trust implicitly in the bufo, as a practically divine representative of nature, but this may sound to some like a romantic notion. Beyond my own personal philosophy, however, I trust in the chemistry of the exchange, which provides a firm scientific basis for experimenting with psychedelic substances. DMT is found everywhere in nature. It has no harmful side effects. It leave the body in less than 30 minutes. Someday, I imagine the venom will become a kind of wonder drug, curing diseases of the body through heart/mind reunification. No doubt it was used by indigenous peoples for this very purpose long before this priceless information became available to the world in the 1970s.

In my three weeks of tripping an average of once a day, I have experienced familiar tropes of death and resurrection. I saw the light and went up into it. I thought the light was gone forever and gave up all hope of ever seeing it again, as I believed at the time that light and dark are essentially the same. Yesterday, I smoked 7 times over several hours in the afternoon - one time too many, judging by the wasted smoke on trip 7. At one point, I felt myself surrounded by my loved ones, and everyone was there, smiling at me, because they already knew everything. I imagine or feel or see Ana, Hydro, my parents and grandparents, aunts, uncles and cousins. It is as if I realize or remember our oneness, or unity, our love and pride. I am surprised to see them, but they saw me all along.

Again, with this vision or fantasy, I assume at some level that this is it, I've finally gone too far, dying, dead. Each ending seems like the final one, so I give up and let go. Each time I am surprised to wake again, or return to ordinary consciousness, realizing that I don't know what just happened, and it is important, the most important thing that has ever happened to me, because it is the closest to now, and has brought me fully and completely back to the present moment. My ignorance is revealed to me anew each time. The mind must know it's humble place, in service, learning.

Many phrases occur to me, repeatedly, as I plunge deeper and deeper into the Self, my self. I often use them in songs and poetry to remind myself of their value to me. Here is a partial list:

Let it be what it is and not what it's not.

Give up existence.

The poet's passage.

I turned myself inside out for you.

Actually, it's both, and neither.

Go into it. Go deeper.

This is only the beginning.

Don't get any big ideas.

The devil is a liar.

What you did before, you cannot repeat.

Trust the process.

Face your fears. Embrace them.

Hold onto the present moment.

This is the other side of awareness.

We did all of this for you.

Get yourself together.

Oh, okay.

◉

11.04.18 -- 3 times -- *See blue notebook*

I went to a place very far away. There was only black and white. The bufo is rewiring my brain. I can feel it happening inside me. For forty years, I lived in fear, sheltering me weakness, my vulnerability, my left side. Now I am being unified, made whole, saved from misery. I had to be brave, to face the darkness in me without looking away, and to go into it, deeper, all the way to the other side. I had to abandon comfort, pleasure and light. I had to be willing to die. The same themes recur, over and over, but each time I trip, I am once again surprised to be alive, and humbled to realize not only how little I know, but how little knowledge means in the face of the unknowable. More words add up to less. Smoking less has given me new benefits. My old anxiety is slowly leaving me, a little at a time. In order to be what I am, there is nothing that needs doing. I can simply be me. Words express theory, but love comes from the heart, steady, pumping.

I do not know what happens next, but I came back here, where I know who I am. Now I am more willing to listen, to follow directions. It was the world in me that gave rise to the world outside. Without contrast, we would have nothing. Void is all. Life is a lie. Your story is a fiction and so am I. Emptiness gives birth to all of this. God is meaningless. The time is now to realize…existence…and then we fucking die die die. But what that means, we cannot know, until we cross over, past the point of no return. I, for one, goodbye. Ego, black dot. White field, I yield. Will I return forever to this place I once felt safe? Is there any other place to be, for you me anybody?

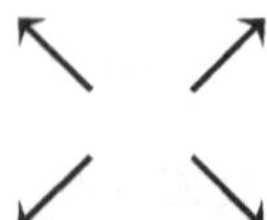

11/05/18 • 4 times

Fasting today, so far, anyway.

I saw the black and white, the yin and yang, the only choice. It's either this life or death with zero hope of anything but coming out on the other side to start all over again and be the other next time. This time I am beyond terrified, feeling I've seen what it may mean to die, to really die, when then end is the end, for all time. Dear God. Hold onto the light. Love all, serve all, black and white. The contrast is all there is, these two basic elements, the either/or, the only choice, one I already made. I believe that if I go into it, I will lose my life and I have no idea what will be on the other side, but the safe bet is death means the end of my existence as an individual, if not the end of this entire universe. Death would mean going through a black how, three days in the tomb, god turns his back, total darkness, complete absence of life and light.

How can I make a choice to do that to myself...when I have no idea what is on the other side? Is this ego death, this suicide? What can I hold onto? What hope can I cling to, going through? Why would I do this thing? What if the end is all there is? What if I can truly die and that is the end of my life?

No redemption, no memory. No heaven or hell. No more me. This is beyond the pale. This is...crazy. Essentially, if I give up my life, I will go through the Big Crunch, and another, Bigger Bang. Closer to the center, this time. A new universe. A whole new canvas, to begin again. The fulfillment of every prophecy. Somehow, this is the meaning of relativity. What about now, this love, this life?

※

11.06.18 -- 3 times

Each time I think I've reached the end, it is only a new beginning. The sun is my third eye, externalized. And yours, too. It's the one thing we all have in common: the sun of God. Fasting this time, 48 hours. Three trips today, outside, inside, outside. This was heaven all along. I let myself forget. Now I get it. Maybe tomorrow will be the end of the bufogenesis experience. Sometimes, I want it to be over. After I trip, things get wavy. I expect my friends to appear, a celebration underway. Maybe I will have to wait, for my wedding, for the year 2020. Coming to terms with this unreal reality is really something special. Life is always new, a constant stream of novelty. When I smoke, I need only remember to relax, to accept what the trip does to me. All my old fears are fading fast. I am being redeemed. Praises be.

11.07.18 -- one time -- Recorded 11-08-18
In the stone courtyard this time. It comes to me
that death is final relaxation. As long as I remain
here, holding onto this body from within, there
may be some tension, if I cannot let go. And only
with a massive hit can I hope to do so,
although…there are other psychedelic plants I've
yet to try, and perhaps each one is a step on my
path to liberation.

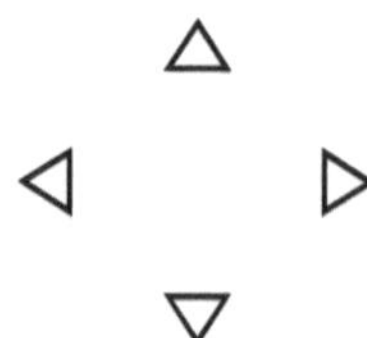

11/08/18 • • • Seven times

Understanding beyond words. A bump on the top of my head. Becoming consciousness. Spirit animates this corpse. I saw the black and white. My world was reduced to seeing everything through the yin/yang. Colors are secondary, but contrast is the secret. Like oil and water, they can be mixed, but the combination is only temporary. All of this, just to dance with you, to see and know and love the other. At one point, I was there, in the garden of eden. I did not even look around to see who was there, although I saw the boy and the dog. It was a perfect place, heaven on earth. But I was focused on the goal, to escape the body through the top of my head. And I did not succeed, perhaps because I was not ready, but I am learning to relax and trust the voice inside, allowing the spirit to move me, the ego who identifies with body. I saw that ego is hollow. There is no me, no solid thing, no entity. I am a hollow reed, like a tree, a vessel for energy.

I spoke in tongues today. Glossolalia. Total nonsense. It was glorious. And I realized that language has no inherent meaning, only familiarity. The key is in the fearless freedom to play with sound, to channel the om from the source. I was there, in that place, all the way there, in heaven. The colors is the yard were primary; green grass, yellow walls, brown trees, orange flowers, black birds, blue sky. And the playful language of babies poured fourth: *"Wa-ta-sha-she-ka-la-bon-da-la-ma-he-ka-lay-no-twee-ka-na-me-tay!"*

But the intuitive understanding of the psychedelic trip doesn't last. When I come back down to earth, and eat and drink, I feel like my old self again. But I am forever changed by that vision of heaven. I will never be the same again. And on the seventh trip today, as the sun set in the west, behind the house, the voice within spoke to me, and it made promises I believe it will keep, if I do my part. It told me to trust it, the voice of spirit. I can stop over-thinking everything, always acting conservatively, out of fear, afraid of being punished for something, for being less than perfect, never good enough. I can quit self-sabotaging based on the false belief that I don't deserve to be happy. If I obey my inner spirit guide, it will lead me to the promised land, and tell me what to do and say to stay on the middle way, to be free to play. The voice said to accept the life I have, to give up seeking something more. It was only my desire that spoiled the perfect life I had; I was overlooking what was right in front of me. We made a deal today. Mind and body will serve the spirit which animates this body. I will get out of my own way. I will let the spirit move through me. I am no body.

《☆》

11.16.18 • 3 times+

11.17.18 • 3 times+

I have begun placing some bufo under my tongue (+) before smoking. This seems to loosen my attachment to the outer layers of the food body and this experience offer new insight into the nature of my individual existence. I think of mind, ego, budhi, atman, brahman.

All around me, life works in synchronistic harmony. If there is a bug in the system, maybe it is me. My thoughts are expressed by people around me. They seem to be tuned into my frequency. Defense mechanisms for maintaining distance are breaking down. Nothing means what it once did. I'm nostalgic for something that never existed. It all makes sense now, if I can face it. Nothing is about me. I exist on a continuum with all living things, united underneath.

We are clouds in the sky, drifting by, nebulous and free, blown by the breeze. We are shadows, dancing. Every night, I die in my dreams. And then I wake up here, again. It's never over. We return to oneness and bounce back. While I feared the darkness, you loved the light. You were right. I find yang in yin and yin in yang. No more fears.

I am living under water. I do not need to breathe. I see so many pretty colors. Gravity keeps me in my place, for now, and I am grateful. Honestly, I'm not ready to leave Earth for the stars. I have so much to learn before I go. I need to cry, but I must fast to feel my feelings. True emotion is too much for little me, but I must persevere. As a humble psychonaut, I will be brave so I may someday show others the way. It's not even about me. I am no body.

11.19.18

Seven times or more.

Bufo under tongue, effective.

Bufo swallowed, not effective.

See notebook, left hand writing.

11.20.18 :: 3X

See notebook. Follow the signs. Listen. The bell rings. Fear is not good motivation. Act from love. Remain in balance. Do your best. Give thanks for every opportunity. One more day of fasting makes three. One more trip into the jungle of my mind. Tomorrow morning. After, Thursday, break fast. Celebrate. Eat well for a week, one meal per day. Notice how proper breathing is easy. Keep your mouth shut. Fasting sharpens your senses. Food will taste better. Colors will be more vivid. Everything will be better because you were willing to give it up. You have 36 hours left. Go all the way. Unify your mind. Know yourself as an integrated whole. Even if it means you have to give up the body and die, trust the process and look forward to the other side, the heaven on earth you were promised. How you see things makes your life what it is. See only good, only God. Sacrifice your self and get born again. Redemption.

11.21.18 • 3X

I am a reincarnation of myself.

Union happens at top of head.

I feel the African in me.

Renounce lesser motives.

Be done with bufo.

No more.

Shelter no weakness.

Harbor no secret need.

I trust you, inner voice.

Expansion and contraction.

Above, below.

Within, without.

Breathe easy now.

Tomorrow is a new day.

Eat, drink and be merry.

Everything in moderation.

Low shall not control the higher.

Feel breath in top of head.

Teach the middle way.

Avoid extremes.

Be a free man.

Don't be moved by fear.

Love is your motivation.

Go forth and sin no more.

God bless you, my son.

You are born again.

Serve the servants.

Get born again.

Like suicide.

Release.

11.25.18 : 3X

Worms, we are, in dirt.

Body-consciousness, hollow.

We eat, fuck, shit, repeat.

Animal instinct.

Disgusting.

11/26/18 --

I have gone all the way to the very edge, to the precipice of life and death. And my death, it waits for me, out of respect, because I stalked it in the same way it stalks me. I do not know what is on the other side, but I know darkness waits for me. I am almost ready to go, to bet on heaven, and immortality. But not quite, not yet, not tonight. I will take at least one more day in paradise. No reason. Free will. Just because I can.

Because ME.

♀

11.27.18: 7 times - 3 day, 4 night
Fascination with desire, on the one hand,
enchants mind with memory, and dooms us to
repetition, addiction and the law of diminishing
returns. Familiarity breeds comfort, protecting
weakness, and becomes contempt if you lose
your edge. But obsession with darkness is the
spell of fear, aversion, the opposite of desire,
running scared. With one of these devils - or
tempters - comes the other. Life is a deadly trap,
and once you're gone, you may never come
back. And the true and final darkness may be
eternal. For me, the middle way is the only way I
can live survive, live and breathe easy. This
moment now makes it all worth it. I gave up all
hope this last time. The darkness, it was sick. It
wasn't funny. I was very sorry. Death closed
over me. I could not help myself, and it took me. I
said things aloud, like about how it was because I
didn't listen that my life was wasted. This time
was my ego death complete. Sick.

Now I'm back. Surprise.

Don't presume to know anything. Remain open.
Do unto others. No memory. Balance fear and
love. See the light in all things.

Holy Mary, mother of god...

11.29.18 - - 3X+
I have reached a level of experience where I no
longer wish to date to share my perceptions. Died
3 times or more. Still alive.

11/30/18
Today is the end of my seven weeks in Mexico. I
might make a list of all the things I saw, learned
and imagined. Now I go back into the past, home
to the enchanted island, with promises to keep,
and dreams to realize. I will honor my chosen
family. I will do me.

12/01/18 - - Final thoughts

Over the last week of this trip of trips, I finally began smoking at night, outside at first, and then the last time in my room, I felt, saw, thought and experienced things which I hesitate to share. Not since childhood have I known myself in this way, from the inside out. What I've been through this last seven weeks is nothing less than a full self-rediscovery. My life flashed before my eyes a hundred times. All the forgotten keys have been recovered, old memories unearthed, wounds healed. The bufo toxin may well be some kind of magnificent placebo, for all I know, but it worked on me, literally. What 14 years of therapy failed to do was put me in touch with my god-self by way of direct psychedelic experience. DMT rolled back the clock for me. I was was reduced to my basic elements. Ego death occurred at least once, the night of my realization of inadequacy and regret: *"Its not funny at all. I don't get to have what I want, because my best wasn't good enough. Oh, no. Oh, no!"* I was sure it was all over. I crossed over into nothingness, eternal black, with no hope of ever seeing light again. Later in the week, in my room, I faced death again, without running away. It is stalking me, yet it waits on me, too, giving me time and space to meet it on my terms. This is a gift I receive, a blessing. And all these people I meet along the way, they look so very familiar, like from a past life I forgot, recently. My assemblage point has been moved, by my friends, to the top of my head, the higher mind. Now I am rediscovering my innocence, intelligence, curiosity, and the body's animal appetites. My instincts are sharper than ever, senses alive and kicking. For all this new life experience, I owe a debt of gratitude to my spiritual family, the people who fuck with me. This is a love I lost and forgot, come back to rescue me. When I turn these notes into a book, I will tell stories in greater detail. Epic. Winning.

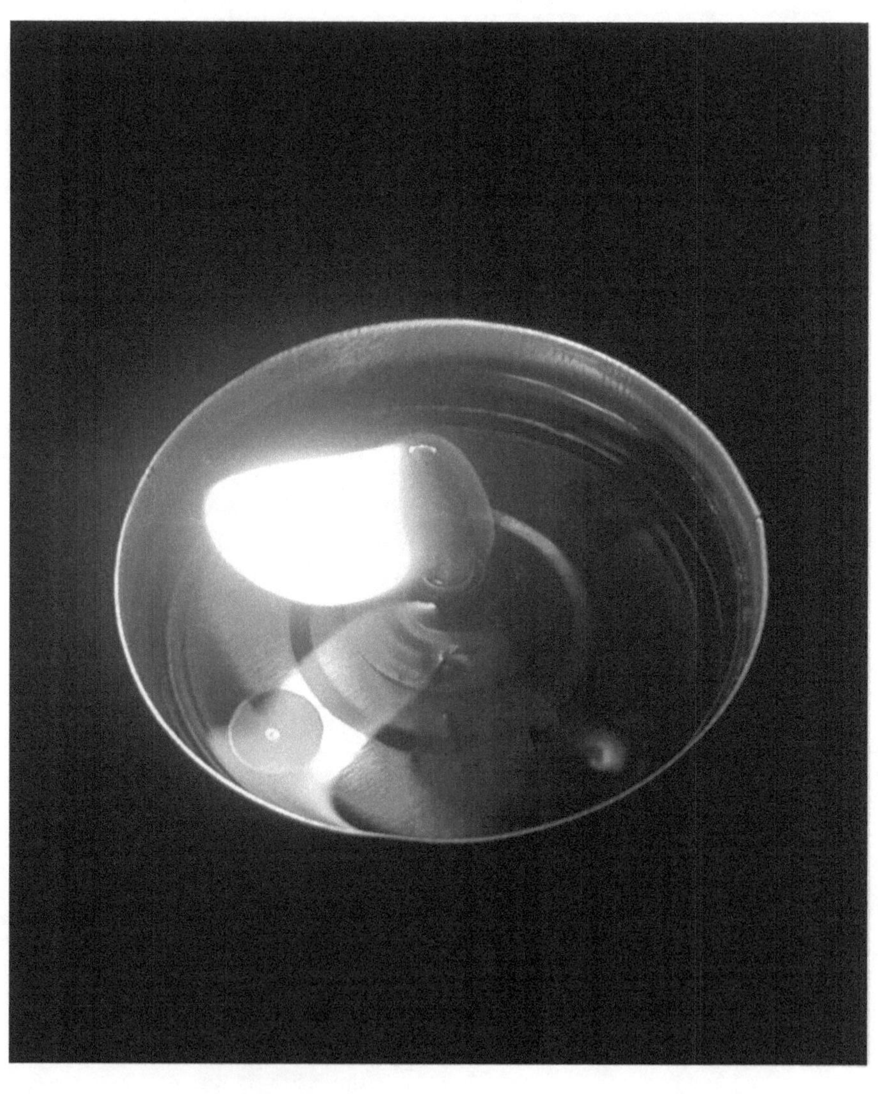

Epilogue

As I reached the end of my seven week retreat, I found myself less interested in recording what I felt and saw, and more interested in the experience itself. There is so much left to say about those last days, but...I want to share it face to face, with people who want to hear about the experience directly. If you have read this far, and want to know more – and, especially, if you are considering the benefits of following in my footsteps, I would be happy to tell you more. Suffice it to say that shit got ridiculous. Only a fellow psychonaut would believe the things I saw smoking all alone, late at night, in the dark. It was enlightening, illuminating, humbling, and terrifying. And even though I thought I was done and gone any number of times, I find myself back here, the same as I ever was, facing the same dilemmas, living the same life I made for myself. How can I sum up for you my seven weeks in Ajijic?

I don't know. It's too soon to say, maybe, what this experience means to me, or how it changed my life. As of this moment, I have been back home in Puerto Rico only two weeks. I can say, however, that if you have reached the end of your rope, and you can't not try this shit, then I can tell you it is worth its weight in gold. That the universe gives us this key, and contains this doorway, it is proof of something. If, like me, you struggle with boredom, apathy and ADHD, with meaninglessness and suicidal tendencies, then the bufo alvarius experience may be just the thing you need to get some perspective on the matrix of modern day living. DMT is not habit-forming or addictive; there are no negative consequences. But it is not for everyone, because, literally, it makes you lose your fucking mind. It's a mind fuck. By smoking the bufo, you surrender control and volunteering for ego death. For anyone considering suicide, I recommend trying this first. After all, you have nothing to lose...right?

• Addendum •

Dear Anamore

Eleven More Steps

Answer Me!

Round Face Girl

Regeneration

Satisfied

New Awakening

Astral Travel

Travel With Light

Honey Moon

Impulse Control

Pep Talk

Dear Anamore

For the first time in ten years
I feel some healthy curiosity
And I don't feel guilty
For being hungry

Since my first suicide attempt
I have been living in a panic
Post traumatic shock
Lifetimes of guilt
Washing over me
Fading away

I can change
I can change
But in one way
I stay the same

My love for you
Holds true
My aim

10.23.18

Eleven More Steps

*I have a problem
And I need help
Either I come out better
On the other side
Or I die, but
Either is better
Than merely surviving
When I can learn
How to have a good time
If I can just stay fine
And it's okay to be afraid
I'm going to get through this
Whatever it is, this
Period of adjustment
My coming to terms
With the past
And letting it go
At long last, finally
Turning the page
After confinement
Nowhere else to go
But free*

10.23.18

Answer Me!

On the wrong side of the wall
If I climb high, I risk a fall
But I cannot stay here
Now that I know the truth
It was never about me at all

There is a battle going on
Between good and evil
For the hearts of people
And I am switching sides
Just in time for war

Put me on the front line!
Let me die for something!
Stand in harm's way!
I need to see the enemy!

In the name of love!
In the name of unity!
Who dares go there?
Who defies the treaty?
I command you!
Answer me!!

10.24.18

Round Face Girl

I met a round face girl
At the beach today
Because she smiled
At my dog, and
In that moment
I knew this was a person
I could love forever
It was insight, at first sight
The light in her eyes
I recognized
From some time
Long forgotten
So I struck up
A conversation
And she told me
She was a witch
And I agreed with her
That men are the pits
So she cast her spell
For my own good
So I could be happy
Serving her, for all eternity
And on that day
We became a family
Us three: : :
The round-face girl
The dog, and me

10.24.18

Regeneration

You can not go back
The way you came
You cannot return
To the life you left
Behind, this time
You have to begin
Something new
And that is the
Good news
Because
What you do now
Will save your soul
From hell and
Damnation
For eternity
Making you
The hero
You need
To be...
Finally

10.25.18

Satisfied

One day, love
I will say goodbye
For the last time
Not soon enough
But all too soon
Nonetheless
Because
It was you
I came for
To eat
Your
Fruit
And
Drink
From
Your
Cup
And
Die

10.25.18

New Awakening

Only the beginning
Getting into winning
Standing under time
A living enterprise
Multiply, divide
Peaceful harmony
Implied at
Higher levels
Of existence
My, oh, my

Holding
Synesthesia
Man, alive
Self-remembers
Being present
Pays attention
To the breathing
Takes a dive
Feeling wavy, baby
Swimming dizzy, lately
Underwater noise
It's the gateway
Drug of choice
For all the
Girls and
Boys…

11.07.18

Astral Travel

Back to the center
And around again
Flat circle time
All evens out
When ends meet
Horizon lines

It's like a disc, this, my space ship
All made of light and very bright
But I am trapped inside of it
With all I need, but no exit
And everything I see outside
Appears to be a mystery
I cannot solve
It isn't mine
To have
Or hold

The choice was made
So long ago
And now I trust
Machines to think
In place of me
And this I call
My being free:
The eye opening
Frequency

11.08.18

Travel With Light

There is so much I do not know
Enough to be afraid or draw
Conclusions, based on evidence
Collected past the present tense

Rules are always
Changing what it means
For me to be alive
And if I live forever
It will be outside of time

Here and now, I must admit
The universe did all of this
And I confess, what worked before
May never serve again
The purposes of men
And therein lies the rub

We require novelty, powering the engine
Brand new information, fueling our reactions
At a subatomic level when
Non-locality is the reality
Surrounding everything
We are not merely
Here or there
But everywhere
In history

11.08.18

Honey Moon

Our scars make us
Who we are
Real and true
To each other
Humans being
In the flesh
Learning virtue
Present tense
It makes perfect
Sense experience
Out of body exit
Coming soon
Enough to wait
To be set free
From the prison
Intellect
Returning then
From west to east
Pilgrims, traveling
Night and day
On hands and knees
Back to the garden
Of Eden, the city, of Zion
My seventh heaven
Where it all begins
Again for you
And i-

11.10.18

Impulse Control

Thinking slows me down
Too much to feel the love
I need to live naturally
So I let go and flow
No impulse control
No regulation
River of life
Runs wild
In me
And I
Pick up
Momentum
Downhill, racing
Water follows gravity
The path of least
Resistance
The easy way
No impulse control
No regulation
River of life
Carry me
Home
Free

11.12.18

Pep Talk

Face it, Jack
You're a hack
Nobody needs your shit
You should just
Up and quit this
Business foolishness
Daydreaming
Waste of time
No more pie
In the sky
For you, kid
Honestly

Get yourself
Together
Act your age
Go to work
Pay the bills
Stay humble
In the cut
On the low
No profile
Grind away
For a while
Keep it real
Until then
Namaste

11.17.18

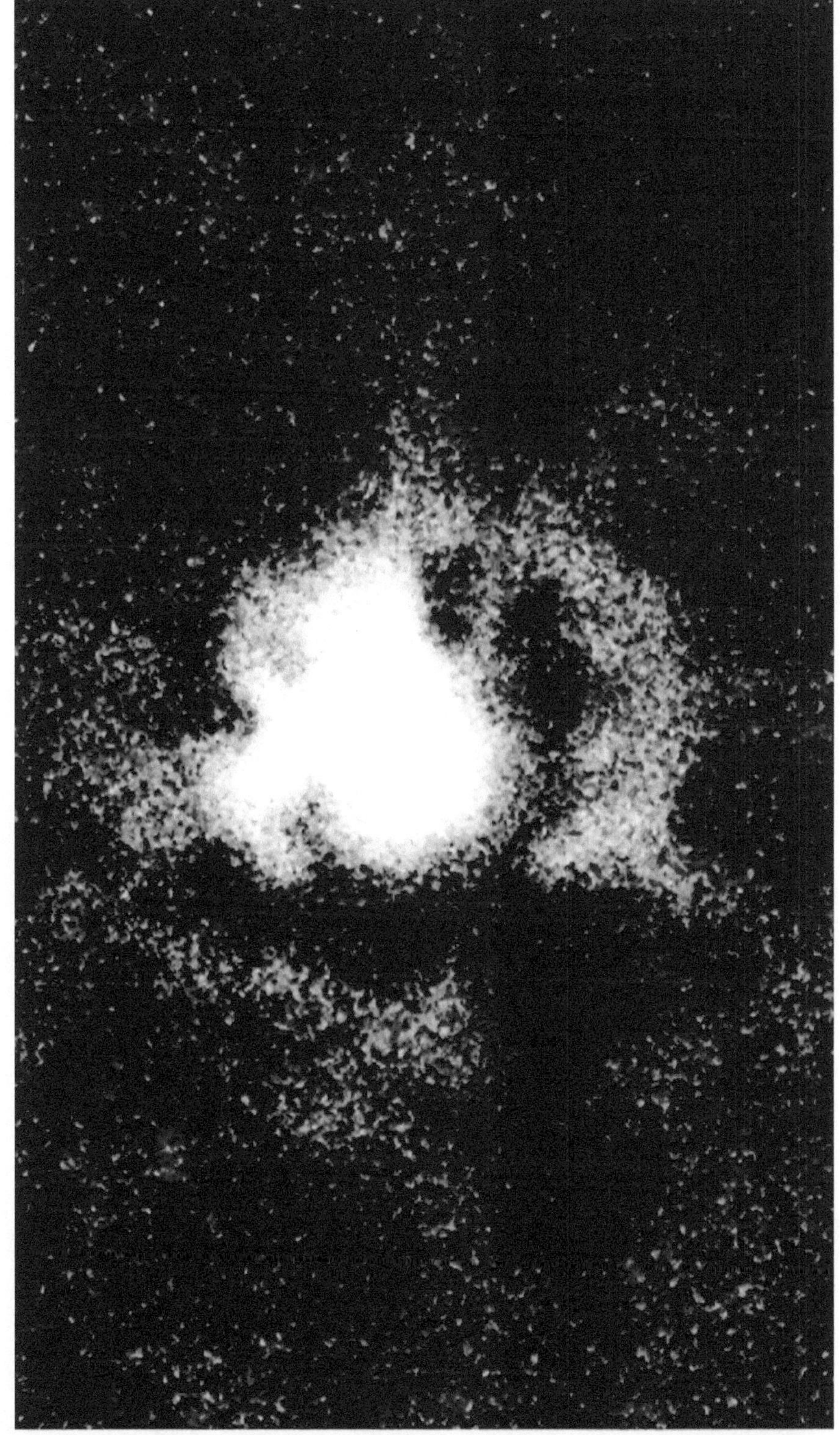

Books by JXS

Conscious Progress

Notes To Self

Words For Music

Hijacking God

Perfect Love

New Poems

Out Of Reality